The Mysteries of Angkor Wat

For Ronnie Mae, Jonah Max, and Daniel Evan

Acknowledgments

The first person I met in Siem Reap was my guide, John Teng. During my many visits to Angkor Wat, he patiently escorted me through the temples over and over again. He quickly understood that I was interested in taking photographs that were not like those always shown in the guidebooks. I am grateful to him and his colleagues, Sok Samnang and Chea Dara. My hosts, Anthony and Fiona, at Villa Siem Reap and the River Garden provided shelter from the heat and rain and lots of advice about exploring the roads less traveled. I was also lucky to stay at the Angkor Village Cultural Hotel and there make the acquaintance of Mrs. Neth and her *apsara* dancers. I thank her for the invitation to visit her school. On each of my visits to Siem Reap I was able to visit the Jayavarman Children's Hospital. I met Dr. Beat Richner, hospital director and cellist, and had the pleasure of attending his weekly concerts. The hospital offers free services to all the children of Angkor, and proceeds from the sale of this book will be used to help them continue to provide medical care. I learned quickly that the ruins of Angkor are vast and their stories are many. I thank Daniel Sobol for sifting through my mountain of notes and photographs, for being a tough editor, and for finding the story in this book. Many thanks to Karen Lotz, Kate Fletcher, and Maryellen Hanley, who have again crafted this project together with me at Candlewick Press. Thanks to Susie Cohen for her counsel and guidance. And, of course, to the many children of Angkor Wat who led me on journeys or sold me cold drinks and fruit on scorching hot days; this book is about and for them.

• •

First edition 2011

Library of Congress Cataloging-in-Publication Data
Sobol, Richard.
  The mysteries of Angkor Wat / Richard Sobol. —1st U.S. ed.
    p. cm.
  ISBN 978-0-7636-4166-5
1. Angkor Wat (Angkor)—Pictorial works. 2. Temples—Cambodia—Angkor (Extinct city)—Pictorial works. 3. Angkor (Extinct city)—Pictorial works.
4. Cambodia—Antiquities—Pictorial works. 5. Angkor Wat (Angkor) 6. Sobol, Richard—Travel—Cambodia—Angkor (Extinct city) 7. Angkor (Extinct city)—Description and travel. I. Title.
DS554.98.A5S67 2011
959.6'02—dc22   2010041479

CCP 16 15 14 13 12 11
10 9 8 7 6 5 4 3 2 1

Printed in Shenzhen, Guangdong, China

This book was typeset in Dante and Interstate.

Candlewick Press
99 Dover Street
Somerville, Massachusetts 02144

visit us at www.candlewick.com

The Mysteries of
Angkor Wat

≫ EXPLORING CAMBODIA'S ANCIENT TEMPLE ≪

RICHARD SOBOL

CANDLEWICK PRESS

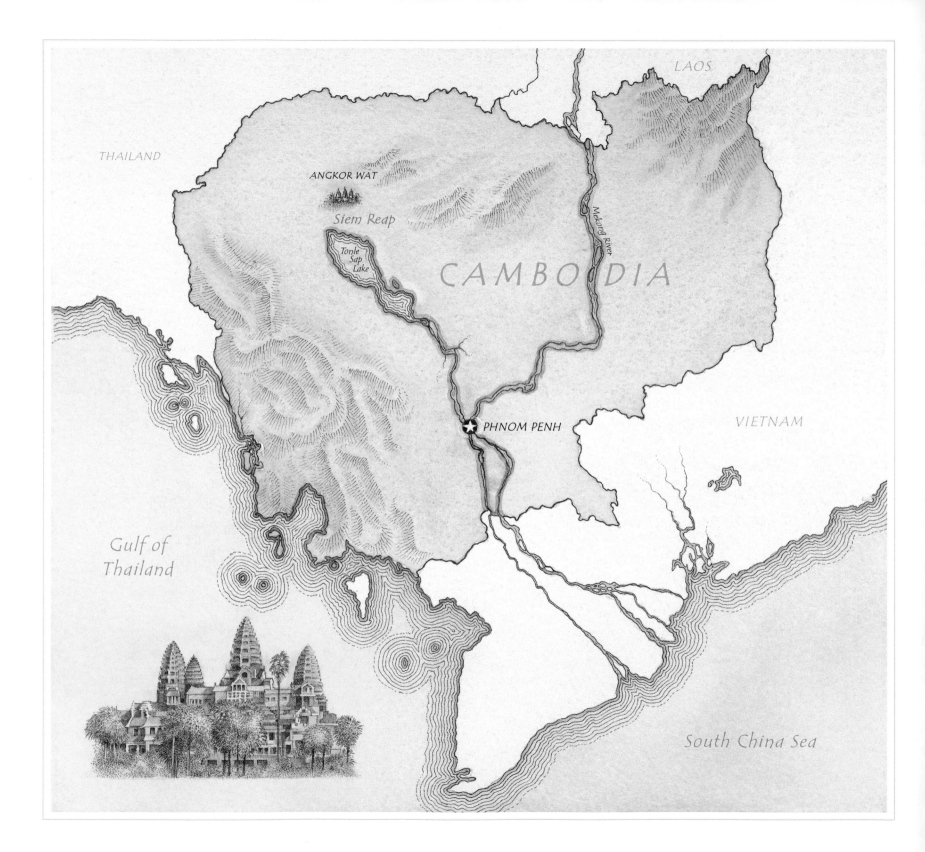

For years I had dreamed of visiting Angkor Wat

and exploring its many ruins. Now, walking through the airport in Siem Reap, Cambodia, with piles of luggage and photo equipment, I could hardly believe that I was about to see it for myself. Although my travels had brought me to neighboring Thailand dozens of times, this was my first journey to Cambodia. Within minutes of being in the country, I realized that Angkor Wat was everywhere around me: an image of it waved across the Cambodian flag that greeted me at customs, it appeared on some of the bills handed to me at the currency exchange, and the airport's gift shops seemed to feature it on everything from T-shirts to key chains to hats. As I thought about the days ahead of me, when I would finally be able to explore Angkor Wat, I wondered what mysteries waited for me inside those ancient walls.

Richard Sobol

Nestled within the steaming jungle and terraced rice fields of Cambodia is the largest religious monument in the world: the temple of Angkor Wat. Now, almost a thousand years after it was built, the temple's crumbling walls are all that remain of the once-mighty Khmer Empire. Theirs is an unfinished story, one without a final chapter to explain what happened to those who lived here for more than four hundred years. The beauty and detail of the art and buildings left behind, together with the riddle of the fate of those who created them, make this one of the most important and mysterious ancient sites in all of Asia.

While preparing for my trip, a friend told me that John Teng was the best tour guide in town. I got in touch with him, and he boasted that he would pick me up at the airport in his brand-new car. When I arrived in Cambodia and walked out of the airport, I was surprised to find a cheery man holding a sign that said MR. RICHARD SOBOL, waiting for me next to . . . a worn-down old-style Toyota.

After introducing myself, I asked John where his new car was.

"Oh, Mr. Richard. This is it. Only twelve years old, in fact—it is one of the newest cars around here!" A smile spread across John's face, and we both burst out laughing, "You see, for a place with a thousand-year-old monument, this *is* brand-new!"

I was so anxious to see the temple itself that we drove straight from the airport to Angkor Wat, since it was only about fifteen minutes away. When we arrived at the entrance, the first thing I noticed was a group of children selling T-shirts, scarves, postcards, wooden flutes, and beaded bracelets to groups of tourists. John explained to me that because more than two million tourists

⌃ A girl sells guavas and other fruit in front of one of the temple's entrances.

≫ The money the children make helps to support their families and pay school fees.

visit Angkor Wat each year, the children who live near the temple sell souvenirs in order to make a little extra money for their families.

I noticed that one of the girls was selling a kind of fruit that I had never seen before, so I crossed my fingers that it would taste good and bought a piece. She told me that her name was Sokvi, and as I slurped the juicy, apple-like chunk of fruit (which I later learned was a guava), some of the other children approached me with curiosity and asked about my camera.

When I explained that I was a professional photographer, they screamed with delight and shouted, "Take my picture! Take my picture!"

I chuckled and snapped a few shots.

"My name is Nak. Where do you come from?" one boy asked while I clicked away. When I told him that I was from the United States, he surprised me by saying, "Oh, yes. The U.S.A.'s capital is Washington, D.C.!"

Before I could even say another word, a bubbly girl named Jane asked, "Which state do you come from?" When I told her, "Massachusetts," she proudly told me, "Massachusetts's capital is Boston!"

Then they began rapidly quizzing *me,* asking if I could remember the capital of Kansas, Kentucky, or Oregon. I was amazed! These kids remembered them all—way better than I did!

When I asked how they knew all those states and capitals, and where they learned to speak English so well, they pointed down the road from the temple. That's where their school was, they explained, and asked me to come visit. I promised them that I would visit their class when I came back to see them again. "Before I go," I said, "let me ask you something. Angkor Wat is so big—there's so much to see. What is your favorite place here?"

The kids looked at one another. Nak whispered something into Sokvi's ear, she nodded, and they smiled mischievously to each other. "We have one really special place. If you come back, we'll show you the *dee no soo.* But it's a secret."

I thanked them, told them I would see them soon, and then went with John toward the temple gates. The children waved, and then ran off to greet a group of tourists that had just arrived. As John led me into the temple, I asked him what *dee no soo* meant. Was it a landmark?

The name of a certain ruin? He shrugged and said he didn't know. I wanted to ask him more questions, but when I saw the giant face of the Buddha looming over me as we entered the temple, I forgot about everything else.

Over the next few weeks, I climbed, crawled, and meandered through the ruins, awe-inspired by the splendor of this ancient place.

Angkor Wat itself is filled with mystery. Stretching more than a mile from its east to west gates, it is to this day the largest religious monument in the world. King Suryavarman II built it in the 1100s CE to be the "city temple" for the Hindu god Vishnu. (In the Khmer language, *Angkor* means "city" and *wat* means "temple.") The Khmer Empire was one of the most powerful kingdoms in Southeast Asia for hundreds of years, but then it vanished, leaving

≪ The Bayon temple displays more than two hundred giant carved faces. Scholars think that they could be images of Buddha or even of the king himself.

behind mysteries that scholars would ponder for centuries.

Researchers and scholars alike debate how ancient engineers and workers were able to move the temple's hundreds of large stones and place them so precisely.

⌃ The remains of more than a thousand temples, libraries, and palaces that once stretched across the Khmer Empire still exist. »

≫ After school, children come to the temple to dance among the shadows as the sun begins to set.

Most agree that it would have taken tens of thousands of people to complete the construction. In addition, the temple layout was carefully designed around the sun's movement from east to west between sunrise and sunset. The architects planned where each shadow would fall.

≫ Over time the ceilings have collapsed and fallen into giant jigsaw puzzles of rubble.

⊻ Dancers perform scenes from the *Mahabharata* and the *Ramayana*, ancient Hindu stories.

The Khmer people originally practiced Hinduism, a religion that had been introduced to them by the Indian merchants with whom they traded. At first, Angkor Wat's temples were built to celebrate Hinduism but the king changed the country's official religion to Buddhism in the thirteenth century. Since then, Angkor Wat has been used as a holy site of Buddhist worship.

The Khmer Empire flourished for hundreds of years, but then mysteriously declined in the fifteenth century. What could have caused this powerful, artistic, and creative civilization to vanish? Some think that the Khmer people were attacked by a Thai enemy from the north. Others wonder if the capital city of Angkor was located too close to the Khmers' enemies, so the king and his people moved farther south toward the ocean. Some historians suggest that there may have been a drought and famine or that the nearby forests might have been stripped of all their trees, so no wood was left for building or cooking. To this day, the fate of the Khmer people remains a mystery.

While their homes, stables, and shops (which were built from lumber or other materials) have long since crumbled away, the stones of Angkor Wat have maintained their permanence almost one thousand years later. Though much of the temple remains intact, archaeologists have never

⌃ The temple of Banteay Srei is built from red sandstone. The softness of the stone allowed sculptors to create detailed carvings.

uncovered any artifacts of daily life from the period. Since hundreds of thousands of people lived at Angkor Wat during that time, no one can seem to figure out why there is barely any evidence of their daily life.

Most of the carvings in the temple walls of Angkor Wat display the Buddha or depict Hindu gods and stories, but if you hunt carefully, you can find carvings hidden in these walls that show images of what everyday life for the Khmer people must have been like. I scanned the walls for these carvings, searching for clues about this lost civilization. As I wandered through the stone corridors, the world of these ancient people began to come alive through the sculptures and carvings of families going to market, women carrying water, boys harvesting water lilies, and children playing music. Curiously, as I walked through the streets of contemporary Cambodia, I began to see that these images, although they were sculpted nearly one thousand years ago, are reflected in the daily lives of the Cambodian people still living here today.

》 》 》

A Cambodian woman carries water using the same technique that is shown in these carvings from almost a thousand years ago.

Children tap out rhythms on musical instruments that are very similar to those used by their ancient ancestors.

The carving shows an ancient head massage, which still feels good today!

Lotus flowers are harvested from small wooden boats. Not only are lotus flowers beautiful; their leaves and seeds are also popular additions to stir-fry cooking.

⌃ Every sculpture of an *apsara* dancer is different. The individual artists who chiseled the figures chose the details of their costumes, jewelry, and hair decorations.

More than any other image, I saw over and over again portraits of female dancers etched into the stone. Each one had a slightly different expression, a unique smile or pose. I asked John, my tour guide, about these figures, and he explained that the dancers are known in Khmer as *apsara*. He also told me that children still learn these dances at traditional Cambodian dance schools. He offered to take me to one so that I could see for myself.

As we drove through the narrow back streets of Siem Reap, John told me about the recent war in Cambodia. He spoke softly, almost in a whisper, "You know, Richard, we are just now starting to recover from the war and the deaths of so many people in the 1970s and 1980s. Our teachers and doctors and artists were forced out of the cities during the war, and many other people were killed. During that horrible time, many of our traditional arts and culture were lost," he said sadly. "But," he continued, "that is why it's so important to teach these dances to the children—we want our traditions to live on and be celebrated far into the future."

When we entered the *apsara* dance class, I was instantly struck by the similarities between the poses I had seen carved on the temple's walls and the dances the young children were practicing here. It was as if the stone portraits had come to life before my eyes. I watched as the older dancers helped the younger ones to refine their movements, following complex choreography, which involved precise movements of the fingers and toes and sharp changes in tempo. John leaned over and whispered to me, "These movements have been passed down from

⌄ These poses are based on the traditional Khmer dances of long ago. Teaching them to students helps to maintain the traditions and stories of the past.

generation to generation. Each pose actually tells a story and has a specific meaning. These students are training to act out the same stories that the carved dancers in the temple were telling."

Watching the children rehearse, it was hard for me to imagine what story each dance was telling, but I knew the movements were a language of their own. Although I did not understand exactly what the bending of a knee or backward curvature of a finger symbolized, I could still appreciate the beauty of the dance—the meaning remained a mystery.

≪ It takes many years of training to perfect the delicate poses of traditional *apsara* dancing.

My time in Cambodia was nearing its end, but I was still determined to solve at least one of the secrets of Angkor Wat—the one that the children had promised to show me when I first arrived at the temple. The next morning—my last day in Cambodia—I decided to return to the spot where I had met the children on my first day at Angkor Wat, and see if I could find some answers. But when I got to the entrance, none of the children were there. I asked John where all the kids had gone.

He laughed. "Mr. Richard, in the morning, they go to school— of course!"

John explained that most children in Siem Reap attend school in the mornings and then head to the temples to greet visitors for the rest of the day. Others work in their family gardens or help to care for younger brothers and sisters in the afternoons, when their parents go to work or do business in Siem Reap. The children who do not have enough money to pay the monthly fees for the government school can attend a free school nearby.

Because the temples of Angkor Wat are such a popular tourist destination, even the youngest children understand that learning English will give them a chance for work. They know that learning a foreign language will allow them to interact with these visitors. When they are older, many will work as guides, showing people the mysteries of Angkor Wat.

Every day, the children recite the English alphabet, repeat the days of the week, practice writing their name in English, and learn how to introduce themselves and ask questions like, "Where do you come from?" As well as memorizing the capitals of all fifty United States, they also learn every European and Asian country and their capital cities, too!

I arrived at the school as class was ending. Several of the kids recognized me and ran up to greet me, shouting, "Hey, Mister Photo! Take my picture! Take my picture!"

"All right, I'll take your picture," I said. "But will you show me your favorite place at Angkor Wat now? Today is my last day here!"

≫ Nearby homes are often built from bamboo and banana leaves. Many do not have electricity or running water.

≪ Sokvi and her friends live surrounded by history. Fallen temple stones line the paths to their houses.

They agreed, and after stopping at their homes to drop off their schoolbooks, Sokvi, Nak, and several of their friends and siblings led me across a rice field, past the main temple of Angkor Wat, and down a side road. Now, finally, on my very last day, I was about to discover a mystery that had not been in any guidebook, a special secret that the children of Siem Reap were going to share with me.

The children took me to Ta Prohm, one of the crumbled temples of Angkor Wat that, over hundreds of years, has been reclaimed by nature. Sokvi, Nak, and their friends have played in this temple all their lives. They know these ruins so well that they could show me places that few official guides ever would. Although this temple, overgrown with trees and vines, is a maze of corridors and collapsed piles of stone, they knew every corner, doorway, window passage, and secret chamber hidden within the smooth moss-covered stone piles.

"Where is the *dee no soo?*" I asked Sokvi and Nak for what felt like the billionth time. "Did we pass it yet?"

"Most people walk right by it," Sokvi responded, then lowered her voice and whispered, "But you can photograph it, or else people might think you are crazy. Come on!"

The kids laughed hard as I tried to follow them, slipping and sliding with every step I took. *Where are they taking me?* I wondered. *Have I survived elephant charges, gorilla poop, and hippo chases only to be crushed by a ton of stone in a Cambodian temple ruin?*

≪ As we squeezed through a narrow archway, I saw signs warning people not to enter and to beware of falling stones.

⌃ Throughout the temple, wooden planks are laid out along the popular tour paths, but Nak and Sokvi opt for the soft mud of unmarked trails and the rounded tops of fallen stone slabs, remnants of roofs and walls from long ago.

The trees at Ta Prohm temple are so large that even with my widest-angle lens I can barely fit the entire trunk in the photograph!

Seeing my hesitation, Nak laughed and motioned for me to follow. "This way to the *dee no soo!*"

When we emerged from a narrow passage, I found we had entered an open courtyard filled with groups of loud, sweaty tourists listening to their guides. The sounds of so many different languages being spoken all at once scrambled to create a jumble of sound: Korean, Japanese, Chinese, Italian, Swedish, Indian, British, Irish, Australian, and American tour guides all telling visitors the same information about Ta Prohm.

Ta Prohm is famous among the Angkor temples and well known for the dense jungle and giant trees that have grown up and around its stone walls. Their roots look like the twisted tentacles of a sea monster from a horror movie. Because some of these trees could have been planted when the temple was first built, they may be more than a thousand years old.

Then Nak stopped. "After we collect some food, then we will show you," he said. Because it had rained the night before, there was a

↟From within the deep angled
cracks in the rock, small green
gardens sprout up after a week
of nourishing rains.

blanket of soft green on the stone rubble. These moss-covered stones, many of which have carved stories of the past hiding under the green surface, produce wild vegetables for gathering and eating. I rested while the children filled their bags with the green sprouts and leaves.

Amazed at how the ancient temple could provide food for its neighbors, I thanked Sokvi and Nak for sharing this secret with me. "Oh no, *Meestar Reechar*," Nak said with a grin. "This is not the secret, but it is just around the corner!"

We passed though one more doorway, and I realized that we were near the West Entrance, an area that I must have passed dozens of times during the past weeks. But I had never noticed anything unusual or extra special there. Though the trees were magnificent and the ruins beautiful, this area seemed no different from the hundreds of other spots just like it nestled throughout the temple complex.

≫ My young guides run across the moss-covered stones. Their bare feet grip the slippery surfaces far better than my fancy hiking boots.

↟ Nak and Sokvi brought along this dinosaur toy to help me understand the secret they wanted to share with me.

"This is the place," Nak announced, smiling. "Now, can you find the secret?" I looked around, searching for any signs of why this would be their special place. What was the secret? Then I saw Sokvi reach her hand into her pocket and pull something out.

I looked closer. It was a small, plastic, green-and-white stegosaurus—a children's toy.

All of the children's eyes were on me as I looked at it. I laughed and said, "Come on. You guys are playing a joke on me. Why did you bring that toy here?"

Sokvi looked at me and said triumphantly, "This is here. We have a *dee no soo* at Angkor Wat. You can take a picture!" Still confused, I went along as she, Nak, and their friends walked toward a narrow carved panel in the corner of the roofless room. I moved closer, and saw there, on the wall, carved inside a circle, a creature that could only be described as a dinosaur—a stegosaurus, in fact. Of all the thousands of carvings in the Angkor temples, of *apsara* and Hindu gods and legends, there is one dinosaur, a single carving of a *dee no soo*. I snapped photo after photo, as if to capture proof before it vanished.

I put down my camera and told the kids, "I've been here for three weeks, photographing Angkor Wat, exploring the abandoned temples, and learning about the ancient Khmer people. I have read twelve guidebooks about the temple, and none of them mentioned this dinosaur.

None of the professors or historians or archeologists seems to have written about it, recorded it, or even knew it existed. You all are truly the best guides! Thanks for sharing your secret with me."

The sun was beginning to set, and I had a flight to catch, so they walked me out of the temple to the entrance, where John was waiting in his "brand-new" car. I thanked my new friends again, and as we pulled away, they waved good-bye and held up the plastic dinosaur for

⌄ The children of Angkor Wat were the best guides of all. They knew an amazing secret that no one else had shown me.

>> The *dee no soo* of Angkor Wat is no longer a secret, but it still remains a mystery.

me to see. All the way to the airport, my mind was filled with questions—even more now than I had had the first day that I landed here! Who carved that stegosaurus? How did he or she know about that dinosaur? Is it possible that they had discovered a well-preserved fossil in the steamy jungles of Southeast Asia? Could it have just been an interpretation of a crocodile or some other now-extinct reptile? Or just an image sprung from an artist's imagination?

The dinosaur carving is just one of the many mysteries I discovered during my visit to Angkor Wat. I saw the beautiful work of the people who crafted art from stone a thousand years ago. I also saw many talented contemporary artists, like the dancers who pose and curve their bodies to tell their traditional stories in dance and music. In its past and its present, Angkor Wat is filled with creativity and expression. Maybe one of the many sculptors who lived here in the times of the kings wanted to create this mystery and leave generations to come wondering why this one stone had a symbol unique unto itself—one single carving out of thousands that didn't quite fit in. Perhaps he brought his children here, and they too ran barefoot through the temple to see the secret *dee noo soo*.

It's likely we will never know for sure why a carving of a dinosaur appears on the walls of Angkor Wat, how the majestic temples were built, or why the Khmer Empire vanished. These are just some of the mysteries found within the walls of Angkor Wat.

⌃ Me with my guides under one of the giant trees at the Ta Prohm temple.

Angkor Wat Facts

Since no written or oral records of the Khmer civilization exist, much of the history of Angkor Wat is the result of study and speculation. Many of the facts are still unknown.

Angkor Wat is the largest and most well known of the ruins of the Khmer Empire. This area in northwestern Cambodia and northeastern Thailand was known as Angkor.

The earliest structures of Angkor Wat were built in the 800s. Construction was completed around 1150, during the rule of King Suryavarman II.

The Khmer civilization is thought to have reached its peak in the 1100s and 1200s, when the population grew to at least one million people.

No one is sure why, but the Khmer Empire most likely disappeared sometime in the 1300s and 1400s. After the temples were abandoned, the thick forest grew up around the buildings and hastened the collapse of the walls and ceilings.

There are more than one thousand temple ruins around Angkor. Angkor Wat is the most detailed and magnificent and is said to be the largest religious monument in the world.

There are more than three thousand *apsara* dancing figures carved into the walls of Angkor Wat. Each one is unique.

The ruin known as the Bayon features 216 enormous faces carved into fifty-four towers. Some think that they are images of the Buddha, while others suggest that they are of King Jayavarman VII, the Khmer ruler in the late 1100s.

The early Khmer people were Hindus. In later years, Buddhism became the primary religion.

People from all over the world come to Angkor Wat, and many Cambodians visit during full moons and on Buddhist holidays.

In 1992, Angkor Wat was named a UNESCO World Heritage Site. UNESCO sites are protected and conserved for the good of all humanity. UNESCO stands for United Nations Educational, Scientific and Cultural Organization.

Siem Reap is the nearest town to Angkor Wat. It has many hotels, restaurants, galleries, and shops, as well as a new international airport. The first traffic light went up in 2002, and the first ATM machine was installed in 2005.

In the 1970s, Cambodia had a civil war and the name was changed to Kampuchea, an ancient name for the Khmer Empire. Many people died under the brutal rule of the Khmer Rouge government, which was defeated in 1979, though another ten years of unrest and fighting followed. Peace talks and negotiations began in 1989, and shortly afterward, restoration work began on Angkor Wat. When that was completed, in 1992, the temples of Angkor Wat were opened to tourists. Since then, more than two million visitors a year have come to explore the temples.

⊻ Clay cooking pots are brought to sell in the villages around Angkor Wat. They must be strong to survive a trip over the rough dirt roads.

Glossary

angkor *(AIN-koor)* city; sometimes means holy city

Angkor Wat *(AIN-koor waht)* literally "city temple"; the largest of the temples of Angkor

apsara *(ahp-SAH-rah)* beautiful women; often dancers

Buddhism *(BOO-diz-um)* Asian religion stressing peace and acceptance of others

guava *(GWAH-vuh)* a tropical fruit with juicy flesh and a strong, sweet aroma

Hinduism *(HIN-doo-iz-um)* an Indian religion embracing many gods

Khmer *(kuh-MEER)* the empire that thrived in Cambodia from the 800s until the 1300s; also the name of the language spoken in Cambodia today

Mahabharata **and** ***Ramayana*** *(mah-hah-bah-RAH-tah, rah-mah-YAH-nah)* ancient Indian epic stories

Nak *(nahk)* Cambodian boys' name

Siem Reap *(SEE-um reep)* the town closest to Angkor Wat

◈ A patch of open sand becomes a playground in the shadow of an ancient temple.

Sokvi (*SOK-vee*) Cambodian girls' name

Suryavarman II (*ser-yah-VAR-mahn)* a ruler of the Khmer Empire and the principal builder of Angkor Wat

Ta Prohm (*tah prom*) a temple in the Angkor Wat complex that has been overtaken by trees and vegetation

Vishnu (*VISH-noo)* a Hindu god

wat (waht) temple

DATE DUE